W9-CFW-460

How Animals Shed Their Skin

John— learning more

Enjoy animals!

about animals!

Best wishes,

Betty Tatham

How Animals Shed Their Skin

Betty Tatham

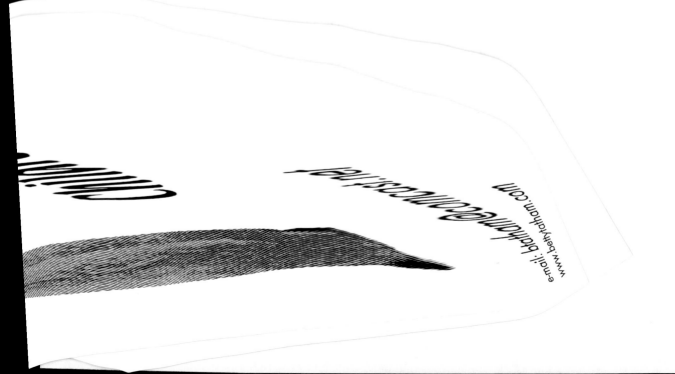

Children's Press
e-mail: btatham@comcast.net
www.bettytatham.com

To Win

Note to readers: Definitions for words in **bold** can be found in the Glossary at the back of this book.

Photographs © 2002: A.B. Sheldon: 36; Animals Animals: 37 (Joe McDonald), 23 (O.S.F.), 18 (Lynn M. Stone); Bruce Coleman Inc./Jane Burton: 24; Corbis Images: 34 (Lowell Georgia), 41 (Wolfgang Kaehler), 14 (Lawson Wood); Innerspace Visions/seapics.com: 12 (Mark Conlin), 5 left, 8, 9 (Michele Hall), 10 (Peter Parks); Minden Pictures/Gerry Ellis: 32, 33; National Geographic Image Collection: 50 (Michael S. Quinton), 20 (Robert F. Sisson), 44 (Brian Skerry); NHPA: 30 (Mark Bowler), cover (Daniel Heuclin); Peter Arnold Inc.: 48 (Doug Cheeseman), 42 (Laura Dwight), 2, 19, 21, 29 (Hans Pfletschinger), 46 (David Scharf); Photo Researchers, NY: 6 (Fred McConnaughey), 47 (Peter Skinner), 39 (Thomas Taylor), 5 right, 26 (Jeanne White); Stone/Getty Images: 16 (Charles Krebs), 40 (Art Wolfe).

The photograph on the cover shows a panther chameleon with its skin peeling off. The photograph opposite the title page shows a snake shedding its skin.

Library of Congress Cataloging-in-Publication Data

Tatham, Betty.
    How animals shed their skin / by Betty Tatham.
        p. cm. — (Watts library)
    Includes bibliographical references and index.
    Summary: Examines how many different types of animals, such as crustaceans, insects, and reptiles, shed their skins.
    ISBN 0-531-12042-2 (lib. bdg.)   0-531-16590-6 (pbk.)
    1. Animals—Juvenile literature. 2. Molting—Juvenile literature. [1. Molting. 2. Animals.] I. Title.
II. Series.
QL49 .T19 2002
573.5—dc21

2001003573

Contents

Chapter One
Crustaceans 7

Chapter Two
Spiders, Insects, and Relatives 17

Chapter Three
Amphibians 27

Chapter Four
Reptiles 35

Chapter Five
Mammals 43

52 **Glossary**

56 **To Find Out More**

59 **A Note on Sources**

61 **Index**

A spiny lobster prowls for food near a rock ledge. This photograph was taken at night with strong electric lights.

Crustaceans

In the shadowy world of the ocean's floor, a lobster crawls out of its hiding place under a rock ledge. Four **antennae** bob on its head, as the lobster searches for **predators**, or enemies. Because it has a compound eye with thousands of lenses at the top of each of the two longer tubes, the lobster can quickly pick up movements of other shellfish, octopuses, or fish. The hairs on its two shorter antennae help the lobster pick up different smells, so it knows if a predator or its next meal is nearby. The danger it faces is from big fish, other lobsters, and lobstermen who set traps. Through the chemical signals it gets through the sense of smell, it can even tell another lobster's mood.

Need to Molt

Like all **crustaceans**, lobsters are animals with an outer crust or shell that has to be shed as they grow bigger. Because they don't have a skeleton inside their body, their outer covering serves as both their skin and their skeleton. It's called an **exoskeleton**. A newly hatched lobster has no claws or legs yet, and it looks like a very tiny shrimp. A baby lobster outgrows its skin and has to shed it or **molt** before it's even one week old.

First, the lobster squeezes some of the liquid out of its flesh to help it pull away from the shell. Then the shell splits between the tail and the body, and along the back shell, and the lobster tugs and pulls until it's free of its exoskeleton. A soft, wrinkled new skin is underneath, and the lobster drinks a lot of water to stretch the new skin. This process takes about a half-hour, during which the lobster's weight increases by 40 to 50 percent. After the new exoskeleton has hardened, it's about 15 percent larger than the old one. Once the lobster has passed the water out of its body, it has room to grow.

At only one month of age, a lobster has already molted three times. While it is still in the **larva** or immature stage, it looks like a miniature adult with four pairs of walking legs and a pair of claws. It is the size of a penny. Soon the claws get bigger and heavier and the lobster sinks to the bottom of the

Near the California coast, a spiny lobster is shedding its shell. Note the exposed soft flesh.

9

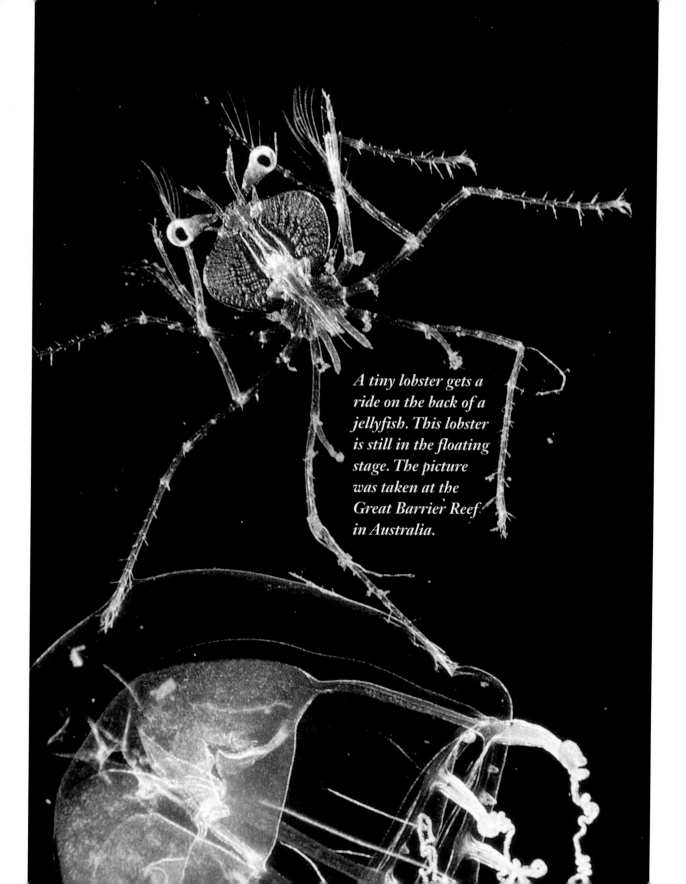

A tiny lobster gets a ride on the back of a jellyfish. This lobster is still in the floating stage. The picture was taken at the Great Barrier Reef in Australia.

Catching Food

A young lobster has many enemies, so it hides under rock ledges, in crevices or caves, or by burrowing down in the sand with only its antennae visible. It spends the first couple of years mostly in hiding, waiting for whatever food might float by.

Older lobsters hunt for food mainly at night. They eat almost anything, both animals and plants that are alive or dead. They catch their food with their large front claws as well as the tiny claws at the end of their first two pairs of walking legs. The two large claws are not identical. The right claw is usually the larger crushing claw, while the smaller, left pincher claw is used for ripping. Some small lobsters even get food from lobster traps. They cleverly enter the traps and eat the bait. Then they leave through an opening that allows smaller sea animals to escape while trapping larger ones.

ocean where it quickly hides. It will spend the rest of its life on the ocean floor.

Lobsters molt about ten times in the first year, three or four times in the second, and less often after that. Once they are about five years old and an adult, they only molt once a year.

Danger While Molting

It takes five to seven years for a lobster to reach its adult size of about 1 pound (0.5 kilogram). That's roughly the same weight as a large grapefruit. Lobsters that live closer to shore or in warmer water grow faster than those that live in very cold water. While lobsters can live to be twenty years or older, most become **prey** or another animal's food before they become adults.

A California spiny lobster is molting its old shell.

Once a lobster has attained its adult shape, molting becomes more difficult because it has to pull out its long legs and big claws from their hard protective shell. The lobster uses its muscles to squeeze out liquid, causing the flesh in its claws to shrink and shrivel to only 25 percent of their former size. The exoskeleton splits between the tail and the body and then along the back shell. The lobster works its way out of the shell by pulling first its body and then all of its legs and claws out of their hard covering.

If one claw or leg stays stuck in the old exoskeleton, the lobster will die. So, to escape, the lobster squeezes a powerful muscle to cut off the claw or leg that can't be pulled out. The claw or leg floats away, leaving a small stump. The lobster's ability to cut off its own **limb** is also helpful when a predator wants to drag it off as prey. Lobsters eat their old shell, and this helps to harden the new one.

Mating and Molting

A lobster and all other female crustaceans can mate only after they have shed their shell, when the new exoskeleton underneath is still soft. When an adult female lobster is ready to mate, her body produces a special **scent** or smell, and she sets out to find a mate. With her claws she fans the scent through the water in front of a large male lobster's den. When the male smells this special perfume, he comes out with his claws held up high to welcome the female. They enter the den and stay there together for a few hours or even a couple of days before the female is ready to molt.

When the time comes to mate, the female lets the male know by putting her claws on the male's head. This is called

Laying the Eggs

The female lobster usually stores the sperm for nine to twelve months inside her body, although she can store them for up to two years. Before laying the eggs, the lobster lies on her back and folds up her tail to make a cup to catch them. She then pushes the eggs from the egg sacs, past the sperm she has been storing. This combines each egg with a sperm before it leaves the female's body. A sticky substance surrounds the eggs and attaches them to the lobster's tail. The eggs will remain glued to the tail for nine to twelve months. (It takes longer for eggs that grow in colder water.) A female lobster can carry more than 100,000 eggs at a time, although the average is 10,000 to 20,000 eggs. The bigger the lobster, the more eggs she can produce. However, only one egg in one thousand will survive to become an adult lobster.

knighting him. It takes several hours for the female to molt. Within an hour after she has shed her shell, they mate. With his first pair of **swimmerettes** the male passes the sperm into an opening in the female's body. The female stays safe and protected in the male's den for about a week.

After her new shell has hardened, the female leaves and they lead separate lives. Mating is the only time that a lobster will be safe from another adult lobster without its protective shell.

Lobsters are one of more than 30,000 species of crustaceans. Most crustaceans live in water. Some, like crayfish, live in fresh water, but most live in the oceans. Shrimp, crabs, and barnacles are some of the better known species. Some are as tiny as a sand flea, while others grow as large as the 12-foot (3.65-meter) long Japanese spider crab. In other words, a spider crab can be as large as a small car. All crustaceans must shed their outer shell the same way lobsters do, as they grow bigger. Like lobsters, they hide from predators, tunneling into the sand or hiding under rocks and ledges while molting. All crustaceans can cut off a body part and grow a new one the next time they molt.

After working hard to weave its sticky web, a spider rests in the center. It may wait there for days or even weeks for its next meal to fly or drop into its spider-silk trap.

Chapter Two

Spiders, Insects, and Relatives

A delicate spiderweb grows as its builder scuttles from corner to corner. Six tiny jets near its belly shoot out silk threads that combine into one strong cable. After the wagon wheel design is ready, the spider returns to the edge of the silk frame. Round and round, round and round it weaves as the circles get smaller and smaller. After several hours, it finally rests in the sticky center. The spider is now ready for its next meal. After the spider has waited for as long as two weeks, the web finally shakes and bounces. A fly has landed. The sticky cobweb holds it, and the spider rushes over. The predator quickly wraps the fly in more silk threads like a mummy, so it can't escape. Then the spider injects poison that kills the fly and turns the inside of its body to mush. Because it can't bite or chew, the spider sucks its meal out of its prey.

Dangers While Molting

As a spider grows bigger, it must shed its exoskeleton. While small spiders only molt a few times, a large female tarantula may have to shed its skin up to forty times in its lifetime.

This spider has molted on some dead leaves. See how its spots match the color of the leaves. This makes it hard for a predator to find while the spider is busy and can't get away.

When its exoskeleton gets too small for a spider, it splits down the back and the spider backs out of its hard skin. Getting its soft, long legs out of their tough covering is especially tricky. If a leg stays stuck, the spider, like the lobster, will die.

Molting is dangerous for many animals because they can't run away from a predator or enemy while they are shedding their skin. It is especially dangerous for spiders that weave webs to catch their food. Instead of hiding in a quiet place, they are easy prey, hanging helplessly in their web for several hours while they shed their old skin.

As soon as a spider has shed its exoskeleton, it breathes in a lot of air to puff up its soft new skin as if it were a balloon, before it hardens. When it breathes out the extra air, there's room to grow. Sometimes it

A spider has just shed its skin. The exoskeleton above it is smaller than the live spider.

19

Scuba Diving Spider

Although most spiders live on land, the water spider—also called the diving-bell spider—lives in fresh water. Since it has to breathe air, it carries a bubble of air wherever it goes. The spider builds a bell-shaped web underwater and fills it with air that the spider collects under a layer of tiny hairs covering its **abdomen**. Like a deep sea diver, it takes its air supply along. The female lays eggs in one of these air-filled sacs. These spiders also molt underwater.

seems that two spiders are in the web, but if you look closely, you may see that one is just the old exoskeleton that has been shed.

Caterpillars Shed and Change

Like spiders and lobsters, caterpillars hatch from eggs. A caterpillar is the larva, or the junior stage, of a butterfly or moth. When a caterpillar's exoskeleton gets too tight, it splits down the back. Underneath the old skin is a new, soft, folded-up skin. The caterpillar wiggles and tugs until it has pulled away from the old exoskeleton. If it tears the new skin, the caterpillar will bleed to death.

Like spiders, caterpillars also breathe in a lot of air to puff up their new skin, in order to have room to grow after the skin has hardened. Some caterpillars also eat a lot of leaves for the same reason.

Before a caterpillar molts for the last time, it produces a small sticky ball so it can attach itself to a branch, with its head hanging down. Then the exoskeleton splits down the back and instead of a soft, folded-up new skin, there's a firm **chrysalis** underneath. This casing protects the caterpillar while it slowly changes into a butterfly or moth. When the chrysalis splits open, the adult insect comes out. It won't grow any more, and so it won't need to molt.

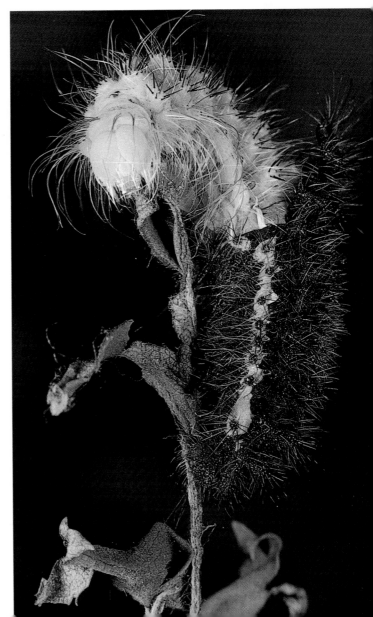

A moth caterpillar has puffed up with air after shedding its old skin that has become too small.

Young Mosquitoes Molt

A female mosquito lays her eggs on water, and they float separately or in small rafts until they hatch. The eggs hatch into larvae called wrigglers that look very different from the adult insects, and their heads hang downward. Each wriggler has two hornlike breathing tubes on top of its head, but if it senses danger, it quickly closes them up and wriggles to the bottom of the lake, stream, or river. When the water is quiet again, the wriggler rises to the surface.

Because they grow very fast, wrigglers have to shed their skin three times in just a few days. As with other insects, the skin first splits down the back before it is shed. Following the fourth and last time a wriggler molts, it turns into a **pupa**, which is shaped like a curled-over comma and has two breathing tubes. The pupa also lives near the surface, but it can still wriggle to the bottom if there's danger. Because it doesn't eat anything while in the pupa stage, it won't grow much and it doesn't molt.

The last molt, when the pupa changes to an adult mosquito, takes place at the surface of the water. After the back of the pupa's shell has split, it pulls away from it and blows the new skin up by breathing in extra air. It takes about ten minutes for the new exoskeleton to harden and the wings to dry. Mosquitoes, bees, wasps, and most flies don't molt once they have reached the adult stage. Mayflies are an exception. They molt once more as an adult when their wings fall off with the old exoskeleton and new ones are underneath.

Getting Ready to Fly

Many changes occur in the pupa stage of a mosquito. New muscles develop, wings grow, and the long sucking mouth gets bigger. Its stomach also changes to prepare the insect to drink liquids. Most mosquitoes live on plant juices, but some female mosquitoes bite animals because they need the protein from their blood to produce eggs.

Other Insects

Grasshoppers also grow in stages. The egg hatches into a larva that molts five or six times. Then it changes to the **nymph** stage, when the insect has no wings. When the nymph molts, the adult insect appears, with tiny wings. It takes about an hour for an adult grasshopper to shed its exoskeleton and wings. It sheds not only its outside covering, but also the lining of its breathing tubes and its **digestive tract**, which digests food and gets rid of waste. A grasshopper sheds this lining at a

On top of the water, an adult mosquito comes out after the pupa's skin has been shed. This is the last time a mosquito needs to molt since it won't grow any bigger.

23

A centipede must molt often. It adds body sections and legs during molts.

time when it gets rid of waste. Cockroaches, praying mantises, and most other insects also shed this inside lining.

All insects have three body sections and six legs. Centipedes, millipedes, and spiders are therefore not insects because they have more than six legs. Spiders have at least eight legs and only two body sections, while centipedes and millipedes have bodies that are divided into many sections, each with at least one pair of legs. The centipede uses its first pair of legs as **fangs** to catch and kill its prey. Its bite can be as painful as that of a wasp. After a centipede has hatched from its egg, it sheds its exoskeleton many times as it grows bigger. While adult centipedes have between fifteen and twenty-three pairs of legs, some species hatch with only seven pairs. New pairs of legs grow in during later molts as body sections are added.

Millipedes have more legs than any other animal—they have between 30 and 202 pairs of legs. When a millipede larva first hatches, it may have only three pairs of legs. Every time it molts by splitting down the back and taking off its old skin, the millipede adds one to three sections with one or two pairs of legs attached to each.

Insects, spiders, centipedes, millipedes, crustaceans, and many other **invertebrates**, or animals without a backbone and skull, belong to the **arthropod** group of animals. Their bodies have at least two sections, and they have more than four jointed legs. Of all the animals on earth, 75 percent are arthropods. Insects are the largest group of these animals. There are more than one million different kinds of insects!

How They Move

Centipedes and millipedes have different ways of moving. Centipedes move the legs on one side alternating with the other side, the way humans move their legs. They look like they're wiggling ahead. Millipedes pull up a whole group of legs on both sides, and then they stretch them out. Their legs make wavelike movements.

A leopard frog blends in with the fern and rock background.

Chapter Three

Amphibians

A leopard frog hops onto a moss-covered rock at the edge of a shallow pond. Its huge eyes follow a mosquito that zooms by and then flies back within reach. With its mouth open, the frog lunges forward. Its long sticky tongue shoots out and traps the insect. The tongue shoves the prey toward the back of the mouth.

The frog can't swallow the way a human does. Instead, it closes its eyes by pulling the clear lid at the bottom of each eye up until its eyes are covered. This pushes the bulging eyes in, and the pressure of the eyes shoves the food down the frog's throat so that it can be digested.

There are more than 3,500 types of frogs. Some live in trees and have thick pads on their feet that help them climb, while others live deep in the ground, but most frogs live in the forest near water.

Amphibians Live in Water and on Land

Most frogs, toads, and salamanders hatch from eggs that are laid in water, and they spend the first part of their lives underwater. At this time they breathe like fish, through **gills** that take in **oxygen**, or that part of the air they need to stay alive, out of the water.

Early in this larval stage, frogs and toads have a large head, long tail, and no legs. Before they become adults and can go on land, they develop lungs and legs. The tails of these **tadpoles** shrink as they turn into frogs that will live on land and in water.

Adult frogs and salamanders have a thin skin that must be kept wet because they breathe through it, as if it were gills.

Frogs That Live Underground

The water-holding frog of Australia lives deep in the ground and comes out just to mate and breed. Its skin glands produce a slimy substance that lines its hole in the ground and then hardens into a clear film. This frog leaves its deep hole only after a heavy rain. To get out, it first has to rip apart the hardened film that covers the entrance. It breathes entirely through its skin. Like most other frogs, it mates and breeds only in water.

Tadpoles live only in the water and they breathe through gills the way fish do. Later on, as adult frogs, they will live both on land and in the water.

Most of them also breathe through poorly developed lungs. However, some frogs and salamanders that live underground or in water only breathe through their skin.

Shedding Skin

Now that it has finished eating its skin, this frog will jump into a nearby stream to sponge up water that will puff up its new exoskeleton and make room for growth.

Because a frog's skin can't grow, it must be shed. When it gets too tight, it splits open on the back and the frog works its way out of it, tugging with its legs. Then it eats the **nutritious** or healthy skin in one piece. The frog works its old skin down into its stomach by shutting its eyes many times, and its tongue also helps push it along.

As soon as it has eaten the old skin, the frog jumps into

Unusual Skin

Surinam toads have an extremely spongy skin. These toads mate underwater, and the male fertilizes each egg after it leaves the female's body. Then he presses the eggs, one by one, into the skin on his mate's back until all of the 60 to 100 eggs are safe. The female carries the eggs around in her skin until they hatch into tiny frogs. She does not shed her skin while her brood is in it.

water where its new skin fills up like a thin sponge. That stretches the skin out and makes room for the frog to grow some more. Frogs have to shed their skin about once a week. Although they can't drink at all, they can pick some water up with their tongue and it then runs down into their throat. However, they get most of the water into their body by sponging it up with their skin.

Amphibians don't have scales, hair, feathers, or a hard outer covering to protect their skin. Most have skin glands that produce a slimy, poisonous liquid that covers their skin and helps it stay wet. The poison also helps keep many predators away.

Toads look like frogs, but, unlike frogs, they have dry skin that is covered with warts. Their lungs are fully developed, so they don't need to breathe through their skin. Toads usually live on dry land, and they spend little time in the water, except when they mate and breed. A toad's skin is much thicker than a frog's, and it doesn't have a slimy covering. Toads have poison glands in their skin that keep many animals from eating them, but they can eat their own skin when they shed it without suffering any ill effects.

Different Kinds of Salamanders

Salamanders look like lizards, but their skin is smooth and slimy and it has no scales. Most salamanders have a long body and tail and four legs. Their skin is thin, and, like frogs, they breathe through weak lungs and their skin. Salamanders also need to live in wet places and some live only in water and never come on land.

Like frogs and toads, salamanders must shed their skin about once a week. Although the skin also splits down the back, it comes off either whole or in pieces. Salamanders also eat their skin.

Sirens are water salamanders that have only tiny front legs and a body that looks like an eel. Newts are another type of sala- mander, and some newts have crested horns on their backs and all the way down their tails. Mudpuppies are salamanders that remain permanently in the larva stage. They never lose their gills, and they live and breed their entire lives in the water.

Shedding their skin is not as dangerous a process for amphibians as it is for some animals that could get stuck and die in their old exoskeleton. However, like all

animals that have to work their way out of the old covering, frogs, toads, and salamanders are more likely to become prey while they are busy shedding their skin.

This newt, like all salamanders, must molt when its skin gets too tight.

A rattlesnake strikes quickly. Its fangs inject poison into the <u>prey</u>, killing it instantly.

Chapter Four

Reptiles

Its skin color and bold pattern blending into the barren desert, a rattlesnake waits motionless for hours. Only its forked tongue moves, darting in and out, in and out, to pick up smells that let it know if food is nearby. Now its patience is rewarded as it uncoils, lunges forward, and grabs its prey. The mouse doesn't have a chance as the rattler bites its head with two long fangs. These special teeth inject **venom** or poison, killing the mouse instantly. Because it can't chew, the snake swallows its victim whole. The rattler won't have to eat again for more than a week.

How Snakes Shed

Before molting, a snake's body produces a milky liquid that loosens the skin and eye coverings so they can be shed. This rattlesnake's eyes have looked blue for several days and now it can't see at all until the exoskeleton is shed.

Each day the rattler grows larger. Its skin can stretch when the snake swallows food, but it can't grow much, so it must be shed. Think of wearing a pair of stretch pants. As you grow bigger, even if the pants can stretch, they can't grow, and so after a while you can't wear them anymore because you can't fit into them.

As a snake outgrows its skin, it has to take it off. When the snake is about two weeks old, its bright, shiny skin turns dull. Although beautiful black diamond markings can still be seen, they are much fainter now. This cloudiness is caused by a milky liquid under the skin that helps to separate the skin from

The photograph shows the dull skin a diamondback rattler has shed and its bright and shiny new skin.

the rest of the snake's body. This white liquid also covers the protective lenses on both of its eyes, which now look milky blue, and the rattler can't see. It spends several days in this dull stage before molting. It doesn't eat anything, and it hides under a rock ledge.

To first loosen the skin, a snake rubs its snout against some tree bark or a rock until the skin peels back from the face and head. The old lenses of its eyes come off with the skin. Now the snake's eyes look black and clear again, and it can see. The snake continues rubbing its skin against a rough surface for fifteen minutes or longer, until it has molted or wriggled out. It takes the old skin off inside out, like a stocking. A shiny, bright new skin now covers its whole body. You can see the overlapping scales in the old transparent skin, called the **slough**. Most snakes molt within the first two weeks of life and every few months after that. When they get older, they molt less often

Hibernating Snakes

Snakes are called cold blooded, but their body temperature actually changes with the temperature of their environment. While humans and warm-blooded animals have a steady, warm body temperature, a snake's body does not. A snake's body temperature is hot or cold, depending on the weather and the amount of the snake's activity. Moving about warms the snake, while resting cools it. In areas where the temperature in winter drops to freezing, snakes **hibernate** or sleep in caves, cracks, under rocks, or in the ground. Hundreds of snakes may pile on top of each other while hibernating in an underground cave. They move very little and they don't eat, so they don't grow or molt.

or only once or twice a year. Molting can be a dangerous time for snakes because for several days they can't see and it's harder for them to escape while they are slowly crawling out of their old covering.

Lizards Eat Their Skin

Lizards have scaly, tough skin that must be shed as they grow bigger. A lizard's scales are different on different parts of its body. Some are smooth, others have a ridge in the center, some are flat and lie next to each other, while others overlap. All of the scales are part of the lizard's skin.

Before it starts to shed, a lizard eats less than usual, and it becomes less active. When the skin gets too tight, it becomes dull and white patches appear, beginning at the lizard's head and later spreading all down its body and along the tail. As the outside layer of skin begins to flake off in big patches, the

lizard rubs against a rough surface to loosen the old skin. It pulls the skin off with its forefeet and mouth, and eats it.

After this anole lizard's skin has come off in flakes, it will eat it.

The skin may look like a dull, thick, whitish plastic wrap, but it is nutritious for the lizard's body. If some of the old skin doesn't flake off, it can cause problems because it can cut off blood supply to the new skin underneath and make the lizard sick.

Different Ways of Shedding

While a snake's scales are overlapping and part of the skin, alligators and crocodiles have scales that grow separately out of their skin, the way a bird's feathers grow. As an old scale rubs or wears off, a new one underneath takes its place. Alligators and crocodiles have a tough, waterproof outer covering for which they are still hunted in some parts of the world.

Skin Can Do Many Things

The skin of some lizards becomes darker in the morning and at night, when it is cool. This helps them keep in body heat because dark colors absorb more heat. Then in the middle of the day, when the sun is hottest, their skin changes to a light color, which reflects the heat or keeps some of it away from their body.

The skin color of chameleons changes to match their surroundings. Some of these lizards also change color to reflect their mood changes. If chameleons are angry, for example, the color of their head changes to yellow and orange. If a male chameleon wants to mate, his head color will turn red, but if the female chameleon is not interested, her skin will have black stripes.

Fortunately, most countries have now outlawed killing these reptiles to make their skins into shoes, belts, or pocketbooks.

Turtles live in the water except to lay eggs, whereas **tortoises** live mainly on land. Tortoises look like turtles. Both have a two-part shell, with the bottom being flat and made of bony plates. The top layer is rounded or shaped like an upside-down bowl, and it's made of horny plates. These plates are joined together to make a hard outer shell that gives the animal its color and markings. A turtle's shell grows larger and thicker by adding new layers from underneath, but the shell never comes off. Turtles do, however, shed the skin on their head, neck, tail, and feet, and it comes off in patches, like a lizard's skin.

Like crustaceans, insects, and amphibians, some reptiles face dangers while shedding their skin. Some can't see for several days, many can't run away from a predator while shedding, and some can become sick and die if their old skin remains stuck. Other reptiles have it much easier. Their outer covering, like that of humans, flakes off a little at a time, and, like humans, they don't even notice it.

A turtle sheds the skin on its head, neck, tail, and feet, but the bowl shaped large shell never comes off.

Humans and all
other mammals feed
their newborn babies
milk from the
mother's body.

Chapter Five

Mammals

The mother of a newborn human baby gently holds her crying child. She smiles as she talks to her baby in a soothing voice until it stops crying. Soon the mother will feed it milk from her breasts. Once it feels full, the baby falls asleep.

All **mammals** are animals that have milk glands. Humans are mammals with two mammary glands, but many animals have four or more milk glands that feed their young. All mammals, reptiles, and amphibians are vertebrates because they have a skeleton and skull, but mammals are the only animals that give birth to live young that drink milk from their body.

Manatees are mammals that live in the ocean. They have some hair all over their body.

Mammals live in different surroundings. Whales, dolphins, sea lions, seals, and sea otters are mammals that live in the ocean, while manatees and dugongs live in both the ocean and fresh water. Seals and sea lions are water mammals that go on land to molt, mate, and breed, but they can only find food in the sea. Squirrels, monkeys, and koala bears are some of the mammals that live in trees, while mice, groundhogs, beavers, and many other mammals live in underground nests or tunnels. Bats are mammals that fly with wings made of skin that is stretched between the long fingers at the end of their forearms. Many types of mammals also live above the ground, such as dogs, cats, deer, bears, and horses.

Mammals have a number of things in common. They have milk glands, they breathe air, and almost all of them have hair or fur. Manatees have stiff, bristle-like hairs about an inch apart over their whole body, whales have one hair or bristle, but dolphins have none. If an animal has hair or fur, you can be sure it's a mammal. All mammals have an outer skin made of **keratin** or dead skin cells that have been pushed to the top by new skin cells that formed underneath. The skin of mammals grows as the animal grows bigger.

Two Layers of Skin

The outside of our skin—the **epidermis**—is made up of about twenty layers of dead cells that will soon rub or fall off. But right underneath this thin, see-through layer, lots of growth and activity are taking place all the time! Here in the much thicker layer of the skin, the **dermis**, millions of cells come alive every second. They have much work to do as they slowly move toward the outside layer, pushing the old, dead cells out of the way. The color of skin also comes from the dermis.

A piece of human skin the size of a large pea, or 0.15 square inches (1 square centimeter), can have 2 million skin cells, 3 feet (0.92 meter) of blood vessels, 100 sweat glands, oil glands, hairs, muscles, and some nerve endings. There are more oil glands, hairs, and nerve endings in some parts of our skin and fewer in others. For instance, the bottoms of our feet and the inside of our hands have lots of sweat glands, many nerve endings, no oil glands, and no hair. The skin is our organ of touch, letting us know when we are hurt and warning us how hot or how cold it is. It also protects our body from harmful germs

Shedding in Patches

Manatees also shed their skin continuously, but the dead skin cells come off in big sheets or patches.

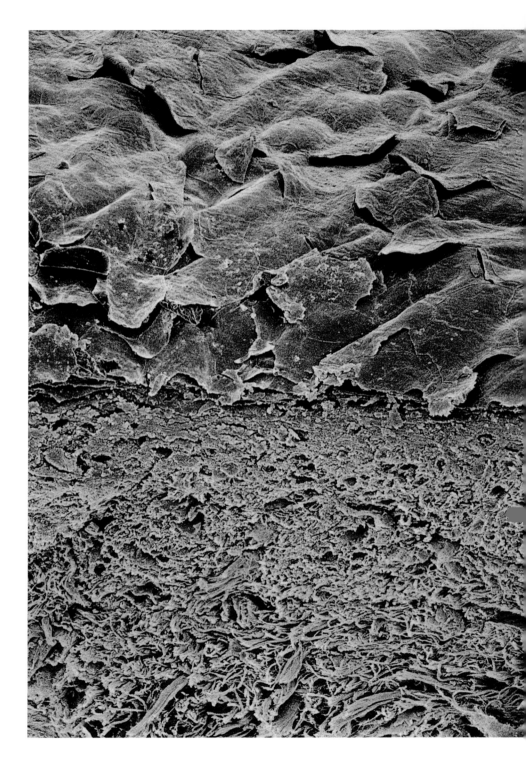

This is an enlarged picture of the top layer of human skin, with the skin seen crosswise.

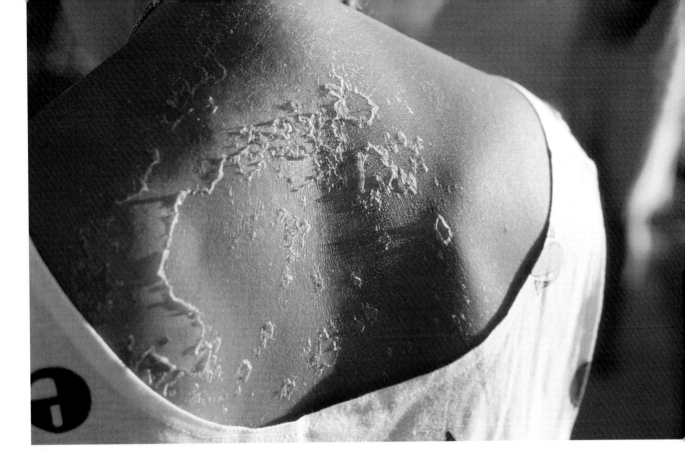

and keeps it from drying out. Our skin has yet another important function: it holds our bones, muscles, inside organs, blood vessels, and soft body tissue together, as if they were in a closed bag.

Although human skin is very thin and can easily be injured by scraping or cutting, some mammals have much thicker skin. An elephant's skin can be 0.25 inches to 1.5 inches (0.6 to 3.8 centimeters) thick, and manatees have wrinkled skin that is up to 2 inches (5 cm) thick and very tough. That's thicker than the length of your thumb!

Have you ever noticed a gray ring around the bathtub after the bath water is drained out? That ring is made up of dead

This woman's back has been burnt by the sun. You can see some of her skin peeling off.

The Skin of Birds and Fish

Like mammals, birds and fish also have skin made of keratin, and it grows as the animal gets bigger. The scales of a fish fall out one at a time, with each scale pushed out by the scale that is already growing underneath. Most birds molt, or lose their feathers, at certain times of the year. Depending on the species, they molt once, twice, or three times a year. Similar to scales and hair, new feathers have already started to grow in the same place when the old ones drop off. All hair, nails, claws, hooves, feathers, fish scales, beaks, bills, quills, spikes, horns, and turtle shells are made of hardened skin or keratin.

skin cells that wash off your body, plus dirt and soap. The "ring around the collar" of your shirt also has dead skin cells and dirt from your neck. Another way you can see skin cells come off is after a sunburn, when large flakes of skin peel off your face or other parts of your body.

It takes about a month for a skin cell to be pushed through the dermis by the new cells that form underneath. When it reaches the epidermis, the skin cell dies and stays there for a while until it gets to the top and flakes off. All mammals shed their dead skin cells all the time the way humans do. They are rubbed off or float away in the air or in water and become dust.

Shedding Hair, Fur, and Skin

There are about 100,000 hairs on a human head, and about 5 million hairs grow on a human body. Each hair grows out of its own small pocket or **follicle** in our dermis. Near the bottom or root of each hair are both an oil gland and a tiny muscle that can make the hair stand up straight or lie down flat. Sometimes when our skin feels cold and we have goose bumps, we can see the hair on our arms stand up straight. Cats, dogs, and many other furry animals also have hair that can stand up straight when they're cold or afraid. Humans are the only mammals, however, whose hair keeps growing all of their lives. But this only happens with hair on a human head and the beard on a man's face.

Humans lose hair all the time, and many other mammals shed their hair the same way, a little at a time. For this reason, it's hardly noticeable. Other mammals, such as weasels and snowshoe hares, change their fur completely twice a year. In the spring, dark hairs grow in and white hairs fall out, right next to each other. The animal always has a fur coat, which changes color from white to mixed or speckled in the spring and then, in the summer, dark fur grows in to blend with the

A snowshoe hare's white winter coat will help it blend into the environment. This makes it harder for a predator to spot the hare.

animal's darker surroundings. In the fall, the opposite happens. The dark hairs fall out, and a thicker, warmer coat of white hairs that's hard to see in the snow grows in for winter. This **camouflage** coloring of animals protects them from many predators, who can't see them. Only animals that live in snow have coats that turn white in winter.

Mammals that shed twice a year grow a shorter, lighter coat that keeps them more comfortable in summer and a thicker, warmer coat with longer hairs for cold winter months.

Thickest Fur on Earth

Sea otters have the thickest fur of all animals. Because they have no fat or blubber under their skin, their thick fur helps them stay warm in the ocean. A sea otter has 85,000 to 1 million hairs in a space the size of a quarter or a circle that measures about 1 inch across (2.5 cm). It has both a thick short-haired undercoat and long hair that covers the undercoat, trapping air between the two layers for extra warmth. A sea otter brushes its fur often to stay warm.

Some animals molt just once a year, in the spring before they mate.

Even those mammals that live in very hot areas have a covering of hair that protects their skin from injury. Lions, tigers, zebras, and many other animals have a covering of short hairs that grow close together. If the animal is attacked, falls down, or brushes against something, its skin is not as likely to be scraped off or otherwise injured because of its hairy coat.

Although crustaceans, insects, amphibians, and most reptiles have to work hard and often face great danger while shedding their skin, mammals are lucky. Their skin grows with them, so they don't need to shed it in the same way as creatures whose covering doesn't grow with their bodies.

Glossary

abdomen—the stomach area where food is digested

antennae—the tubes on an animal's head or body through which it receives information about its environment (sight, smell, touch, taste, hearing)

arthropod—an animal that does not have a backbone or skull and whose body has at least two parts and more than four legs

camouflage—an appearance that will make an animal difficult for an enemy to see, or to fool a predator by looking like something else

chrysalis—the stage when a caterpillar is in a protective hard shell, while it changes into a moth or butterfly

crustacean—an animal that lives in water and has a hard shell or crust for an outer covering

cull—a lobster that has only one claw

dermis—the thick layer of skin that protects and covers our body and is right under the thin outer layer of dead skin cells

digestive tract—the entire system that takes in food, makes it usable for an animal's body, and eliminates waste

epidermis—the outer layer of skin that is made up of dead skin cells

exoskeleton—an animal's outer skin or shell that cannot grow as the animal grows bigger

fang—a long, sharp tooth that is usually curved and hollow through which an animal injects poison into its prey. Fangs can also be canine teeth.

follicle—the tiny opening in the skin through which a hair grows

gill—the breathing organ of fish and other animals that live in water

hibernate—to spend the winter sleeping, usually in a hidden place

invertebrate—an animal that does not have a backbone or skull

keratin—a substance found in the dead cells of the outer layer of skin and in horns, hair, feathers, hooves, nails, claws, and bills

knighting—to turn into a knight, noble person, or animal, or to make special

larva—an insect after it has hatched from an egg and is in the young feeding stage

limb—a part of an animal's body that grows out of its head or trunk, such as an arm or leg

mammal—an animal that feeds its young with milk glands

molt—to shed skin, hair, feathers, horns, and hooves, that will be replaced by new ones

nutritious—food that is healthy for an animal's body

nymph—the last stage of a young insect when it has become an adult but before it has wings

oxygen—a gas that most animals need in order to live, with some breathing it through their lungs, and others getting it from water that passes through their gills or skin

predator—an animal that hunts or catches other animals for food

prey—an animal that is hunted or caught for food

pupa—an insect in a hard casing where it changes from the larva stage into an adult and it does not feed

scent—a special smell or odor

slough—the old skin that a snake has shed and left behind

swimmerettes—limbs of crustaceans that are used for swimming and carrying eggs but not for walking

tadpole—the stage when a frog or toad lives only in water and it has a long tail but no legs

tortoise—a type of turtle that lives on land

venom—poison, such as the poison of a snake

To Find Out More

Books

Cerullo, Mary M. *Lobsters: Gangsters of the Sea*. New York: Cobblehill Books, 1994.

Cogger, Harold G., Ph.D. and Richard G. Sweifer. *Reptiles and Amphibians*. New York: Smithmark Publishers, Inc., 1992.

Editors of Grolier Reference Group. *Amazing Animals of the World*. Danbury, CT: Grolier Publishing, 1995.

Facklam, Margery. *Creepy Crawly Caterpillars*. New York: Little Brown and Co., 1996.

Matchotka, Hana. *Outstanding Outsides*. New York: Morrow Junior Books, 1993.

Miller, Sara Swan. *Radical Reptiles*. Danbury, CT: Franklin Watts, 2001.

Schlaepfer, Gloria G. and Mary Lou Samuelson. *Pythons and Boas: Squeezing Snakes*. Danbury, CT: Franklin Watts, 2002.

Organizations and Online Sites

Animal Diversity Web
http://animaldiversity.ummz.umich.edu/
This online site provides a wealth of information on animals and was created by the University of Michigan's Zoology deparment.

Kids Go Wild
http://www.kidsgowild.com
Created by the Wildlife Conservation Society, this online site for young people provides interesting facts about animals, games, and information about conservation.

National Geographic Society
http://www.nationalgeographic.com
The online site of this nonprofit scientific and educational organization provides information on animals, science, and geography and includes a special section just for young people.

National Museum of Natural History
10th St. and Constitution Ave., NW
Washington, DC 20560
http://www.mnh.si.edu/
From this museum's online site, you can learn more about animals mentioned in this book and take a virtual tour of its collection.

Videos

Hidden Worlds: Frogs, Dragons, Lizards, Monkeys. PBS Home
  Video.

Webs of Intrique. Washington, DC: National Geographic
  Society, 1998.

A Note on Sources

Before deciding to write a book on a particular topic, I always go to my local free public library to explore the subject. The first thing I wanted to know was how many books have already been written on "How Animals Shed Their Skin." When I couldn't find any by that title, I knew that I would probably have to do a lot more research than usual. However, the lack of books also suggested that there was a need for a work on this subject.

While researching this topic, I visited public libraries near my home as well as in New York City, Philadelphia, Princeton, and Trenton, and I checked out the Interlibrary Loan System. I read books on many individual animals, groups of animals such as crustaceans and reptiles, and on human skin. When I couldn't find enough material on insects molting, I continued my research at the Biology Library at Princeton University.

As I finished each chapter I mailed it to my friend, Doug Wechsler, a biologist who directs the Visual Ornithology Department at the Academy of Natural Sciences in Philadelphia. Doug reviewed each chapter for scientific accuracy, and his comments were very helpful to me. My editor later asked a second science expert to critique the manuscript.

I usually browse the Internet while researching subjects for my books and have listed some of my favorite online sites in the To Find Out More section. I love doing research almost as much as the actual writing. This book was especially fun for me because at times it seemed like I was doing detective work as I sought to find out just how these animals shed their skin and how dangerous it is for some of them to molt.

—*Betty Tatham*

Index

Numbers in *italics* indicate illustrations.

Alligators, 39–40
Amphibians, 27–33
  frogs, *26*, 27–31, *29*, *30*, 33
  how they breathe, 28–29, *29*, 31
  poison, 31, 32
  salamanders, 28–29, 32–33, *32–33*
  toads, 28, 31, 33
  where they live, 28
Arthropods, 25

Barnacles, 15
Bats, 44
Bears, 44
Beavers, 44
Birds, 48, *48*

Cat, 44, 49

Caterpillars, 21, *21*
Centipedes, 24, *24*, 25
Cockroaches, 24
Crabs, 15
Crayfish, 15
Crocodiles, 39–40
Crustaceans, *6*, 7–15, *10*
  mating, 13–15, *14*
  molting, 8–9, *8–9*, 11–15, *12*
  replacing body parts, 13, 15
  size of, 15

Deer, 44
Dogs, 44, 49
Dolphins, 44, 45
Dugongs, 44

Elephants, 47

Fish, 48
Frogs, *26*, 27–31
  how they breath, 28–29,
    29
  mating and birth, 28, 31
  number of types, 28
  predator, 27
  shedding skin, 30–31, *30*
  tadpoles, 28, *29*
  underground frogs, 28

Grasshoppers, 23–24
Groundhogs, 44

Hibernation, 38
Horses, 44
Humans, *42*, 43
  color of skin, 45
  hair, 49
  shedding skin, 45–49, *46*
  sunburn, *47*, 48

Jellyfish, *10*

Koala bears, 44

Lions, 51
Lizards, 38–39, *39, 40*
Lobsters, 7–15
  floating stage, *10*

growing a new claw, 13
hunting for food, *6*, 11
life span, 11
mating, 13–15, *14*
molting, 8–9, *8–9*, 11–15,
  12

Mammals, *42*, 43–51, *50*
  common traits, 43, 44–45
  milk glands, 43
  shedding, 47–51
  skin, 45–49, *46, 47*
  where they live, 44
Manatees, 44, *44*, 45
  type of hair, 45
Mayflies, *22*
Mice, 44
Milk glands, 43
Millipedes, 24–25
Molting
  amphibians, 30–31, *30,*
    32–33
  caterpillars, 21, *21*
  centipedes, *24, 25*
  crustaceans, 8–9, *8–9,*
    11–15, *12*
  grasshoppers, 23–24
  mammals, 45, 47–51
  mosquitoes, *22, 23*
  reptiles, 36–41, *36, 37, 39*

spiders, 18–20, *18*, *19*

Monkeys, 44

Mosquitoes, *22*, *23*

Mudpuppies, 32

Newts, 32, *32–33*

Poison
   and amphibians, 31, 32
   and snakes, *34*, 35
   and spiders, 18

Praying mantises, 24

Replacing body parts, 13, 15

Reptiles, 35–41
   alligators, 39–40
   crocodiles, 39–40
   dangers while shedding,
     41
   lizards, 38–39, *39*, *40*
   snakes, 2, *34*, 35–38, *36*,
     37
   tortoises, 40–41
   turtles, 40–41, *41*

Ring around the collar,
   47–48

Salamanders, 28–29, 32–33,
   32–33

Sea lions, 44

Seals, 44

Sea otter, 44, 51

Shedding. *See* Molting

Shrimp, 15

Sirens, 32

Snakes, 2, *34*, 35–38
   hibernating, 38
   shedding, 36–38, *36*,
     37
   as predator, 35

Snowshoe rabbits, 49, *50*

Spiders, 17, 24–25
   molting, 18–20, *18*, *19*
   as predator, *16*, 17–18
   water spider, *20*

Squirrels, 44

Sunburn, *47*, 48

Tadpoles, 28, *29*

Tigers, 51

Toads, 28, 31, 33

Tortoises, 40–41

Turtles, 40–41, *41*

Weasels, 49

Whales, 44, 45

Zebras, 51

About the Author

Betty Tatham is the author of *Penguin Chick*, a science book that was published earlier this year. She has also written *How Animals Communicate* and *How Animals Play*, two upcoming Watts Library books.

Betty Tatham has a Bachelor of Arts degree with a major in Sociology and a minor in Science. As executive director of the YWCA of Bucks County for more than ten years, she designed and implemented many tutoring and other educational programs for children, including the E-Mail Authors Club. This program matches fifth grade aspiring authors with senior citizens to whom they e-mail their story every week. She has received numerous awards for her YWCA and volunteer work. In 2001, she received the Bucks County Women's History Month Award from 19 women's organizations. Betty Tatham lives in Holland, Pennsylvania, with her husband Win.